"Heather's words awaken one's soul, reminding us to take time, not only to reflect, but to question the deeper meaning of things in the universe. Sharing her stories with my two children not only allowed for family togetherness, but opened the doorway for further exploration of the world around us. Thanks Heather for sharing your stories with us."

Shannon D. (Montessori Teacher
& Mother of two children)

"Her stories make you really, really think hard about everything around you. Her stories paint pictures in my head. You should look closer at everything you see. From the smallest bug to the biggest mountain."

Ryan – age 9

"You will be surprised, touched and invited into a way of experiencing your life that will feel like a breath of fresh air. If you need encouragement to open your heart to life, this book will surely move you in that direction. If you have pondered the true meaning of life, in these pages you will find answers from a fellow explorer who has discovered marvelous treasures on the path. Seen through Heather's eyes the ordinary events of our life can become extraordinary opportunities filled with possibility."

Alison Normore, PhD

STORIES FROM THE HEART:
THE LADYBUG WISH

Experiencing Creation from a Different Way of Perceiving

HEATHER A. OLIVER

BALBOA.
PRESS

A DIVISION OF HAY HOUSE

Illustrated by: Alison E. Canty Photography by: Heather A. Oliver
www.heatheraoliver.com

Balboa Press books may be ordered through booksellers or by contacting:

Balboa Press
A Division of Hay House
1663 Liberty Drive
Bloomington, IN 47403
www.balboapress.com
1 (877) 407-4847

Because of the dynamic nature of the Internet, any web addresses or links contained in this book may have changed since publication and may no longer be valid. The views expressed in this work are solely those of the author and do not necessarily reflect the views of the publisher, and the publisher hereby disclaims any responsibility for them.

The author of this book does not dispense medical advice or prescribe the use of any technique as a form of treatment for physical, emotional, or medical problems without the advice of a physician, either directly or indirectly. The intent of the author is only to offer information of a general nature to help you in your quest for emotional and spiritual well-being. In the event you use any of the information in this book for yourself, which is your constitutional right, the author and the publisher assume no responsibility for your actions.

Any people depicted in stock imagery provided by Thinkstock are models, and such images are being used for illustrative purposes only.
Certain stock imagery © Thinkstock.

Print information available on the last page.

ISBN: 978-1-5043-4091-5 (sc)
ISBN: 978-1-5043-4092-2 (e)

Balboa Press rev. date: 10/26/2015

Dedicated to
M J

CONTENTS

A SPECIAL INVITATION
FROM THE CHILD WITHIN EACH OF US

Each of us has experienced a time
when we were or still are a child.

Perhaps some of you will say, "I still am a
child. I have always been a child."

Whether you remember being a child, whether you know
the child within or whether you are now rediscovering The
Child Within, there is something very special about being
a child!

The child sees the Earth and explores life from a place of
wonder, innocence and openness.

Many people who are now adults may say they never had
a childhood like that.

As a child I soon learned that the world was not as open
as I was. Now as an adult I am reclaiming the joys I did
experience as a child and I am choosing to experience my
life now with joy and peace.

I was recently introduced to a wonderful organization that
is helping families with children have FUN! Many of these
families have never been on vacation as one or some

of their wonderful children were born "challenged". The family's focus has been on surviving from day to day. Having a vacation seemed like a dream too far to be reached!

BuddyCruise.org is bringing this Dream to reality for families in the US and Internationally.

BuddyCruise.org creates a vacation with something to offer for all ages and abilities. They provide educational resources, awareness, and promote inclusion for individuals with special needs and their families. Families from North America and from around the world have participated in these wonderful cruises.

I invite you to give a donation from your Heart to this organization.

Please research BuddyCruise.org and perhaps you may even find yourself volunteering or your family coming onboard to volunteer and have FUN too!

I hear the call from the child within you to Be Joy and have Fun with your Life in the most wonderful and beautiful way possible!

BuddyCruise.org

Thank you,
Heather Oliver

FOREWORD

Stories from the Heart: The Ladybug Wish by Heather Oliver

It is with great pleasure that I prepare you for the delights that await you in the following pages. You will be surprised, touched and invited into a way of experiencing your life that will feel like a breath of fresh air. If you need encouragement to open your heart to life, this book will surely move you in that direction. If you have pondered the true meaning of life, in these pages you will find answers from a fellow explorer who has discovered marvelous treasures on the path. As someone who shared some of these experiences I can bear witness to their truth.

I first met Heather in the spring of 2003 when I moved into the building where her massage clinic was located, which was right across the hall from my new office. In her I recognized a healer and kindred spirit, and we have shared many peak moments and sacred journeys over the years since. While Heather might call me her teacher, it is also true that she is mine. Her capacity to live open-heartedly, with trust in her intuition and the universe to guide and support her, is nothing short of remarkable. Her willingness to take enormous leaps of faith inspired me to do the same. In that she has been my role model. So when

I was called to move provinces and follow a new vision for my life, she was there to help and support, to load my belongings and two cats in her van and drive me to the eastern edge of the country. On this grand adventure we call life, I am proud to call her co-conspirator and friend.

Heather approaches life with a presence and openness that is rare. She has at least as much, if not more than her share of challenges and disappointments. Yet these have not, as they might have, caused her to become jaded or bitter. Like the gold that is forged in the alchemist's hands, her trials have refined within her a quality of childlike wonder and joy, a generosity of spirit, unerring belief in the benevolence of the universe and the purpose of her life. That is the thread that runs through these stories, a gift of support to connect us with the source of creativity and intuitive wisdom, to listen to and trust the guidance that is always available.

These stories from the heart are also a powerful reminder to notice the beauty and magic that surround us. They help us remember that no matter how it appears, we are never alone. In these snapshots Heather shows us how the natural world conspires to awaken us to the miracle of our existence. Seen through her eyes the ordinary events of our life can become extraordinary opportunities filled with possibility. As she says, all we need do is pay attention and look for the message. Her perspective is born of the innocence of one who has lived life well and discerned its deeper meaning. These stories arise from that rich well of life wisdom. I know and trust they will uplift and inspire you as they have me.

Alison Normore, Ph.D.
Bonne Bay, Newfoundland and Labrador
March 2015

PREFACE

Have you ever observed a rainbow arching skywards above the sun?

Have you ever watched clouds to see what shapes they form?

Have you ever had a wolf smiling at you?

Have you ever found yourself in the circle of a rainbow? Did you find the "Pot of Gold"?

Heather is a very "heart sensitive" person. She believes in the best for each living being. She has intentionally developed her skills of perceiving creation to guide her on her life path. For most of her adult life, Heather has done her best to both listen within and observe the natural world.

As a young child, Heather perceived the world quite differently. She was challenged in ways that often left her confused and frustrated. Heather was not athletic or dexterous. She often misheard what people said. She considered herself to be not very smart even into her teenage years. Also while Heather loved being in nature, she was fearful of it.

After many years of exploration, she has come to have a greater trust in and appreciation for the value of personal experiences. Heather realized years later that she was highly sensitive and naturally intuitive.

While observing the natural world, she realized many times that there were messages given to her. When she paid attention, she received messages from the call of the Jays, to the flight of a Heron and even from a Wolf.

Hence she is more at one with her environment and realizes that there are messages available at all times. The invitation is to know how to perceive or understand the messages.

You are invited to read the stories within Stories From The Heart: The Ladybug Wish and to observe as they potentially open your perceptions of the natural world and what meaning they might have for your life experience.

The author comes from a line of ancestors who believed in listening for wisdom from Dreams, Visions and the Natural World.

Heather shares some of her early life to empower you to share your story. If you have not shared it yet, perhaps you will reconsider. You may not realize that your experiences may inspire another in a very profound way and give them assurance, inspiration or confidence to step forward into "Life more fully". Whether you speak it, record it or write it, please consider sharing. We may not realize how powerful we really are, and Heather believes that we all really do want to have a fantastic experience while living here on Planet Earth!

Heather trained as a Pre-school Teacher (1978). Years later, while raising her 3 children, Heather acquired further education in the field of Registered Massage Therapy (1997).

Over the years, she has received significant training in the professional energy therapy field – Reiki Master, Therapeutic Touch, EFT, Heated Stones Relaxation Therapy, The Reconnection TM, Reconnective Healing TM, Axiatonal Alignment Therapy, Munay-Ki Rites (Peruvian Teachings), Quantum Touch TM, The Wonder Method TM, Professional B.E.S.T. Practitioner, I Ching Systems Tools.

As a young child, Heather received her first appreciation for the natural world from her parents and her grandparents.

Later during Heather's mid-adult years she received some First Nations' teachings. She learned how the seeker focuses on being connected and feeling in harmony with nature and all life. Heather received teachings about receiving wisdom and insights that both guided and affirmed her way of seeing with her own healing Medicine Walk.

In this book, Stories From The Heart: The Ladybug Wish, you may observe the term, Uncle. For Heather, Uncle means my teacher or my mentor. When Heather wants to give a wise person who walks the First Nations' path respect, she may say, "Thank you, Grandmother or Thank you, Grandfather." This implies someone with wisdom and who shares the story. For Uncle and Aunt, it is more personal. These are "my teachers" versus "the teacher" (Grandfather and Grandmother).

Heather Oliver, RMT, a registered massage therapist, has her own practice at "Healing With Nature's Touch" in Guelph, ON.

Between 2001- 2005, Heather experienced a significant re-awakening that has been evolving and expanding. This deepened her spiritual walk with new insights and awareness. All of these experiences have helped the author to more fully re-remember her natural intuitive abilities.

An avid photographer, Heather enjoys taking pictures in nature! Some of her photography is included in Stories From The Heart: The Ladybug Wish.

Heather is a Canadian who has done some extensive world travel – Europe with her parents when she was 16 years old; across Canada in both directions; to the USA,

Costa Rica, Cuba, Nicaragua, Peru and the Caribbean Islands. Heather enjoys travelling.

Some of Heather's massage therapy clients will be familiar with these stories. She shared her travel experiences and sightings over the years with them.

As she sought inward guidance as to what to write, Heather was reminded of those stories she shared with her clients and found that the stories were just at her fingertips waiting to be put into written form.

The title has been partially explained. What about the "The Ladybug Wish" part?

Further in the book, there actually is a story called, "The Ladybug Wish". Heather wanted to express some of her playfulness and joy with people. She felt prompted to choose this Story to be part of the Title, for it is uplifting and light in nature. The picture on the cover, which was created by her daughter, Alison, conveys that there is something in here for all ages and for your Family.

Heather was sharing about, "Stories From The Heart: The Ladybug Wish", with one of her clients (the mother of a 7-year old daughter and a 9-year old son). The client shared that this book will be wonderful for the family to read together, as the stories invite a deeper awareness of the natural world and help encourage both conversation and observation.

Heather has published works in the "Daily Bread Devotional Book (1985-1992) through the Community of Christ Church".

She created an Instructional DVD for Heated Stones Relaxation Therapy for people to learn how to give this therapy.

Heather also created a Calendar with her photography, including a short explanation of the photos, in 2012.

Heather lives in Guelph, ON. She is a proud mother of 3 adult daughters and a happy grandmother!

The next step was to publish her first book!

ACKNOWLEDGEMENTS

First, I want to thank you, yes YOU, the person who is reading Stories From The Heart: The Ladybug Wish right now! If you read only one of the stories I wrote and it touched your heart in some way, then Stories From The Heart: The Ladybug Wish is a success! So thank you very much! May each and every one of your days here on Planet Earth be wonderful for you!

I would not be writing these stories if it had not been for the help of so many souls from my Guides, my Angels, and all the people who believed in me and encouraged me. You know who you are and I am in deep gratitude.

Thank you Mom and Dad for being the best parents! I love you both very much!

Thank you to my wonderful children, for being patient with an emerging Mother who, I am quite sure, more than challenged you through the years. I am so proud of each of you and I love you so very, very much. I have a grandson now and he unto himself inspires me!

To my brothers who looked out after their little sister even when she may not have been aware, I love you so much!

I want to convey a special "Thank you" to my friend, M J, who inspired me in the first place 12 years ago. Both M J and Dan Frederick helped with the editing of this book and shared some great enhancing ideas for which I am most grateful.

The illustration of the Ladybug on the front cover and all the beautiful illustrations in Stories From The Heart: The Ladybug Wish were drawn by my wonderfully talented daughter, Alison E. Canty! Alison, thank you for your time and dedication to help out your Mom with her dream! I love you so very much!

My dear friend and mentor, Alison Normore, PhD, thank you for writing the Forward for Stories From The Heart: The Ladybug Wish and for suggesting that I explore Hay House Publishing – Balboa Press Self-Publishing! I have found my Publishing Home with these wonderful people. You are such a great inspiration, Alison, thank you! My heart soars!

I want to especially thank all the people who read my manuscript: M J, Dan Frederick, Lois McMillan, Shannon D., Verna Rose, Patti Johnson, Betty and Allan Leeder, Dale Adamson, Carolyn Riddell, Chris Pohlkamp and Lisa Browning. Thank you for your wisdom and insights in helping Stories From The Heart: The Ladybug Wish come more fully to life!

There are two photographs taken by Sandra Irons and Mauro Mavrinac. Thank you for giving me your permission to include these photographs. Thank you, Dale Adamson for helping me understand dpi for including my photography.

I am so grateful for my Church family and friends, to my Heritage re-enactment family and friends, my GIN Network friends, to Ken's meditation group friends and to the Profit Point 17 Class friends.

To all my friends, I am so thankful for the gift of your friendship, beyond and beyond!

The amazing team and staff of Balboa Press Self-Publishing, a division of Hay House Publishing Inc., I am so fantastically grateful for all the great suggestions and wisdom you shared to help Stories From The Heart: The Ladybug Wish to come to fruition! Thank you so very much and with deep gratitude!

Be Your Joy!

Heather

INTRODUCTION

In this book, Stories From The Heart: The Ladybug Wish, I decided to add a little extra exploration for you.

I realize you may enjoy reading these stories and, for you, the stories may draw up memories of similar experiences or new awareness of what you observe and experience. It is my hope that Stories From The Heart: The Ladybug Wish will open up a new wonder for you - to create possibly a deeper appreciation for the natural world you live in and open you further to new insights of wisdom.

When you explore Stories From The Heart: The Ladybug Wish from front to back, you will observe two pages that have all of the titles of each story (after the Epilogue). If you are a tactile person this activity may be something you will enjoy doing. My suggestion is for you to remove these pages and separate each title so that you will have a pile of 27 pieces of paper. Place the story titles in a re-sealable bag. Choose a title, read the story and reflect on the questions provided. Yet another way is to open the book at any point and then read the first story to your right, or be creative to your left. This is intended to create a fun and enriching way to experience your day with new insights or reminders of ways to have fun and joy!

Many of the stories are messages unto themselves. I also invite you to step out to explore some of the activities. One example is to go cloud watching, or to find beauty in what may not seem a beautiful day or environment.

When you are ready, have fun with some of these activities, to help shift your day and empower your life into new ways of being!

Come now explore our natural world with renewed wonder! It is waiting for you to participate.....

Heather Oliver

PROLOGUE - CROWS

While I was out for a drive with a good friend, I remember noticing some Crows in a nearby field and made a comment about them. At the time, we were travelling along some country roads near Waterloo, ON.

I shared a little of what "Crow" means to me. Some of its natural characteristics include how one crow will be on guard duty while the rest look for food. They take turns doing this. In a forest they will give out a "warning call" when something unknown has arrived.

There is an area in southwestern Ontario where battles took place back in the early 1800's. I have observed large numbers of Crows in this area. My sense is that the Crows represent many of the ancestors who gave their lives there.

My friend said, "This is what I want to read about, Heather. I want to read about what you see and observe." This is a paraphrase of what I remember my friend saying to me. She shared that she did not see these things. As I shared, I brought the countryside to life for her. It gave her insights into her life that she had not considered before.

What does the Crow mean for you? Have you ever observed one in flight or sitting on a fence post? Have you been awakened by the song of the babies in their nest? Was it a sweet sound for you?

STEPPING OUT

One day, while I was at the home of Uncle, he and another friend began sharing memories about their forest adventures. I perked up and began to listen, in case they happened to share some wisdom that might help me.

First, Uncle shared a story about being in the bush hunting moose.

Wow! He must have been way up North as that is where the moose live. That forest has bear, coyote, wolf and other 4-legged animals! How brave of him to go into this bush.

I wanted to get brave enough to stay overnight at a family member's cottage on my own. I also wanted to feel free enough to walk on the land with ease and joy!

For me this was still no easy task, because I carried with me what seemed like a mountain of fears. Everything in my rational mind said there was nothing to fear and that all would be fine. However, when I was ready to step out into this reality, it was a whole different story!

Here I was, wanting to go, and still feeling very fearful. I knew the land had all that I needed for the Medicine Wheel I was planning to make. My dilemma was still at hand.

I listened. I suddenly realized that Uncle never did get any moose because the mosquitoes and black flies literally drove him out of the forest! His friend shared a similar story. It was the mosquitoes that drove him out of the bush.

Hmm...I pondered over their stories. Well, if all that they experienced in the bush were black flies and mosquitoes, I knew I could handle that. There really was no need to be afraid.

With these visions now in my mind's eye, I took the leap. I began to make plans for my trip to Bruce County. I already knew there had been no "bear" sightings in years. At the time, it was more about the coyotes and the wild dogs. I had not heard of any of these sightings either. Pretty calm country. Yes, just what I required!

I must say I was excited knowing that I was going to do this. On my own at that! I arrived early in the day. This way I would have time to gather some of the items and feel my success in stepping out right away.

As I strolled along the embankment well above the river on this beautiful warm sunny day, I felt the peace needed for this venture.

My view was spectacular from my vantage point! I paused long enough to step closer to the edge of the embankment to bask in the scene. Around me were the tall pines my Dad had planted over 20 years ago. Across from the meandering Saugeen River was a magnificent field of rich green corn.

Suddenly, I heard a distinctive rustling sound ahead of me and slightly to my right. Startled, I stopped! All the old fears came rushing up inside me. I even had a slight sweat sensation. I froze!

From where the sound had come, out jumped a rabbit. It hopped into more cover. I had startled a small rabbit. It was likely more afraid of my presence. I was much larger than the rabbit!

We had both "frozen", waiting to see what would happen, if anything. It was as if the Universe was showing me, "You will see a harmless rabbit: cute, brown and furry to boot!" I was actually able to chuckle as I headed towards the trail that led down to the river.

Upstream, on my side of the river, was a cropping of deciduous trees. The tall grasses along the river bank swayed back and forth as the gentle breeze moved through them. A gull was soaring by, following the flow of the river. Mmmm...calm again and at peace! I headed on my way.

Do you remember a situation that startled you? A time when you stepped on something only to discover it was a stick or a small branch. Have you been surprised by the sudden movement in a wooded area? You realized just as quickly it was a bird.

"Enjoy Your Day....It is Yours to Create!"
(Bruce M.)

Do you see the Angels in this picture?

BLOWING ANGEL KISSES

Just before I planned to go home one evening in November, I decided to pick a Fairy Card. It came from my Doreen Virtue card set. I picked the card that said, "Daughter". One message from this card is my daughter will have an answer to my question.

Well, I read on and observed that it is important to let the "Inner Child" play. It also said, "An Angel who is like a daughter to me is communicating with me." Hmm...I pondered.

I left to go home. It was still very warm. I sensed my "Inner Child" wanted to go for a walk. I walked around the parking lot thoroughly enjoying the warmth while gazing at the starlight.

The walk was just what I needed. I felt great for doing it! I got into my vehicle and started towards home.

While I was driving through an intersection, I observed an overhead street light go out. For fun and with the energy of my "Inner Child" in my heart-mind, I decided to send it a "Kiss"!

So I did!

Suddenly the light beside that one went out! I blew a kiss to it too! Just in case it was my Angel saying "Hello" to me!

Well, who would have figured! The next two lights went out! I blew more kisses. This is such fun! I observed the ones now behind me come on again.

As I drove along the street, more lights went out! I was laughing and blowing more kisses! Some lights stayed out and some came on again!

In total, 10 street lights had popped out as I drove home! I felt exhilarated and totally joyful! What fun and totally off my radar screen!

I figured the Angels were totally having fun tonight and they so enjoyed the "Kisses"!

Have you ever considered blowing "Kisses" at lights when they pop out? Maybe do it just for the fun of it!

Be The Joy You Are!

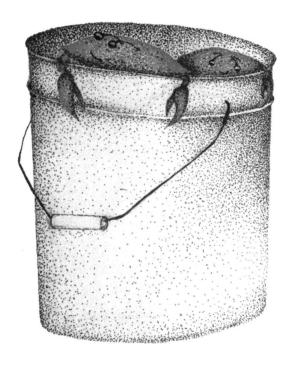

A PAIL OF CRABS

A friend and I were discussing some aspects of life, when he told me a story about how life was for him and the people he knew. He asked me to imagine a pail that has Crabs in it. The Crabs did not want to be in the pail and they were trying to leave. However, every time a Crab came close to getting out, another Crab would pull it back in again.

He said this is how it happens for him and what his life is like.

I listened to his story and then asked him to imagine another story. In my story, I saw the same pail and the Crabs that wanted to leave it. However, I saw the Crabs climbing up to create a pile until the ones on top were able to reach over the upper lip. I continued to see them help each other, like that of a living bridge, so that even the last Crab was able to climb out to leave the pail.

A few years after that conversation, I met the young man again. He shared with me a vision he had. The only thing was, nobody had offered to help him with his idea. Later that same evening I pondered what he had shared. It reminded me of the story he had told me of the pail with the Crabs. He was reaching toward the upper lip; he wanted out.

I was grateful that I had extra money available to give him, when I saw him the next morning. I wanted my friend to have an experience like the "living bridge" from the Crab story, of someone believing and supporting his dream. With the cheque in hand, I gave it to my friend and shared that I supported him. My friend was surprised. I also said that it was a gift, and I did not expect him to return the funds.

Here is his dream.

My friend had recently met an artist who had the skill to draw the likeness of both Tecumseh, Shawnee War Chief and Sir Isaac Brock (Both known from the War of 1812).

The artist had given my friend the designs to work with and the artist gave them to him for free! With the designs in hand, the vision came to put the prints onto tee-shirts and long-sleeved shirts for sale during the 200 Year Anniversary of this War.

It would take money. I did not really know what was needed. When I asked from my heart-place, I sensed that the amount I gave my friend would be enough to get him started!

In August the following year, I saw my friend. He gave me half of what I had given him, as he decided to put up some of his own money. I was happy for him and pleased that he had decided to go through with his dream!

When I saw him the next year, he had completed his vision!

I also met the artist who was truly pleased that his designs had gone to print! Later I received one of the long sleeved shirts. My friend also gave me the rest of the funds and more as a thank you for supporting and believing in his dream.

What impressed me the most though, is my friend decided to not make any extra money from his dream. Instead he gave away the rest of the shirts along with the instructions to make more of them so that all the funds would go to support the youth activities at Fort Malden in Amherstburg, ON.

A lot more Crabs are working together now to get out of the bucket and stay out!

Have you ever felt like you wanted out of a pail and did not see a way out? Do you have memories already about having the "living bridge" experience?

What would your Pail of Crabs story be about?

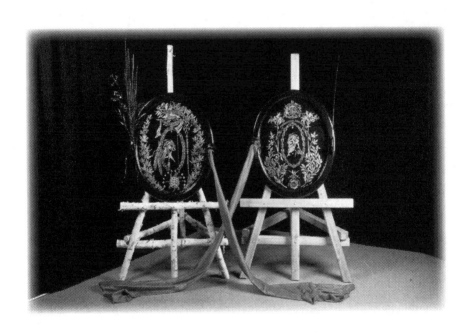

Tecumseh and Brock, created by Mauro Mavrinac.
(Photograph given with permission.)

Do you remember from years ago when you said to another, "Sorry or I am sorry or please excuse me."? The kindly person said, "No problem." Then more recently we heard, "No worries."

Here is what I say to people now. "**All is well**."

I invite you to try it on for size!
(Heather O.)

WOLF SMILE

It has been a pleasure to visit the Halliburton region of Ontario over the years. During one of my visits to the area, I went to the Wolf Centre. (About 8 years ago from this publishing.)

Most of the Wolves were lying in the shade as it was a hot summer day. I stood in front of a window, quietly observing the Wolves.

As I stood there that day, I wondered if the Wolves knew we were there and if they knew where I was standing. It would be a great place for a photo, I thought.

Usually the best view was from a circular, all glass windowed observation room. On this day, I found myself standing in the long hallway to the right of it. At the time, I was the only one in the hallway. It also had windows; however, they were smaller in comparison!

While I observed the Wolves, I saw one rise up and stretch. Then, much to my surprise, this Wolf sauntered over towards where I was standing. When she was directly in front of the window, she turned and faced me.

Now, if it is possible for a Wolf to smile, this one did! I was in awe and astounded! With this opportunity, I took a picture of the Wolf. I silently voiced my thank you to the Wolf. She then turned around to return to her resting place in the shade.

Well, I received my answer and a great picture of the smiling Wolf! That was one amazing experience for me!

What do you think happened that day? Have you ever considered asking questions from your mind?

Smiling for the Joy of it!

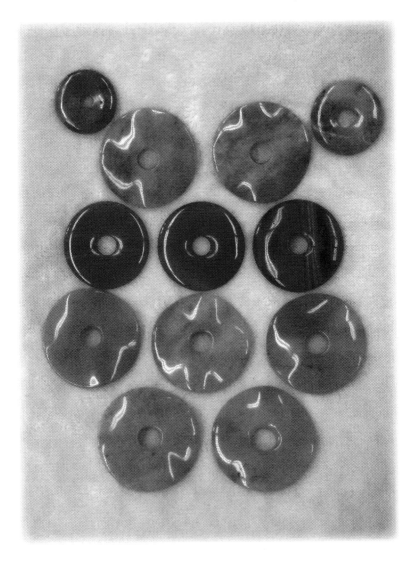

Pi Stones are used when receiving the Munay-Ki Rites.

RAINBOW DELIGHT

The Rainbow has been very special to me for many years. I do not even remember when I became so fascinated with them. I have memories of enjoying them as a child and being curious about where they might end. I was told there is a Pot of Gold at the end of a Rainbow!

In the First Nation's tradition, there are Elders who have spoken about the time of the Rainbow Children or the Rainbow Warriors who are actually the Peacemakers. The time of warring is over, and the call of the Elders is to help these new children be empowered to live from the place of peace.

In the spring of 2008 through to early 2009, I had the opportunity to learn some Shamanic Teachings from a woman who became a mentor when she moved to the office space across the hall from my massage therapy clinic.

This lady had studied Peruvian Shamanic Teachings with a teacher in the USA. This teacher recently told his students to go ahead and begin teaching and sharing the Munay – Ki Rites as they had been taught.

As I read from my notes, I observed once again that here is another tradition that calls for healing our Rainbow Body.

This fully had my attention, as tears came to me with my strong connection to the Rainbow.

Through the years after my training in the field of massage therapy, I began learning about different forms of energy therapies. One of these I studied was Reiki. Reiki is a Japanese energy therapy where students learn about balancing the chakra system that contains all the colours of the Rainbow. I also learned more about our chakra system over time.

I really enjoyed learning and deepening my own spiritual path. I have found opportunities to share some of the information with my clientele and friends.

However, I just did not feel ready to mentor the Munay-Ki Rites.

Finally in early April of 2009, I felt ready to proceed. First though, I wanted to be well organized and versed in what I was to be sharing and giving to potential students. As I read over the information, I was astounded by the connection with the Rainbow. These Rites are about healing, balancing and recharging our Rainbow Body. (It has been shown through Quantum Physics that everything is vibration, including our bodies.)

I spent a few hours preparing for the course I planned to mentor. Shortly afterwards, I gathered some framed pictures that were to be donated to a local charity event. I needed to place them in my vehicle.

As I opened the back door of my van, I observed a Rainbow image on the window. I looked around and was not able to see where it was coming from. When I closed the door, I noticed the Rainbow still reflected on the window. Again I looked around; nothing. The car next to my vehicle also reflected Rainbow colours.

I wondered. Where was this coming from? I did not seem to be able to find or see its point of origin.

In my head I asked, "If you are visible, guide me to your location." I sensed, "Look up." I looked up. Way up. There was the Rainbow! It was above the sun with its curves circling skyward. Truly amazing!

I raced to find my camera! I wanted to take a picture of it, if it was still there. As it turned out, I was able to take two pictures! The one with a Rainbow smile has the mist of a cloud with it. This picture looks like a puppy dog's face with a Rainbow smile for its mouth!

As I continued to stand admiring this wondrous sight, another tenant from the building came out. She asked what I was looking at, and all I could do was smile and point. When she realized what she was seeing, she shared that she had never seen anything like this before and that it had totally made her day!

I had my confirmation to proceed with the mentoring.

Have a look at this picture on the back cover.

What have been your experiences when you see Rainbows? Have you ever seen a Rainbow that is shaped like a smile?

Be the Joy!

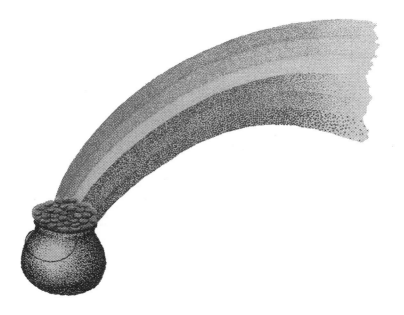

POT OF GOLD

In August of 2008, I decided to attend a Shamanic event in Newfoundland.

Our group had the pleasure of staying at a lovely B&B that was located at the far north corner of a small village community. The B&B dining area faced due west with a sandy beach directly in front of it.

Later in the week, our group was having an early morning breakfast with other people who had also stayed at the B&B. I was sitting facing the water which is known as the Gulf of St. Lawrence. I so enjoyed gazing at the ocean. I live on the mainland and the closest body of water is several hours drive away.

As I gazed, I thought: "Who knows… I might sight a whale or dolphin passing by."

What I saw that morning was a magnificent full arching Rainbow! It spread from one end of the village cove to the other end. As I sat there observing this view, I wondered where the end of the Rainbow was.

Instead what I saw was a reflection of the Rainbow on the water. I followed its course to discover it came to the beach, continued on the sand, and went to the right of the B&B I was in! Hmm....I pondered this for a bit.

Then I wondered about the far side and looked to see what I might find. Sure enough it reflected on the water and up onto the beach to disappear just beyond the south end of the village. (It went beyond my view.) Well, I pondered this too, and then I realized the whole village including the B&B was within the circle of this Rainbow!

I could not be silent. This needed to be seen by all in the room. Yes, all! Even the people I did not know. I got their attention and then showed them what I continued to see.

A lady to my right said, "I thought there was a Pot of Gold at the end of the Rainbow!" I paused for a moment and then silently I placed my hands over my heart.

She said, "Oh, I get it!" She smiled as if to say, "Our hearts are the Pot of Gold!"

I nodded my head.

Had the Rainbow not been so large, I would have loved to take a photo. Frankly, to be in the circle of this magnificent Rainbow was more than a gift in itself!

What would it feel like for you if you found yourself within the circle of a Rainbow?

RAINBOW & LIGHT ORBS

On the evening of July 1, 2009, close to sunset, I was on my way home from visiting a friend in Fergus, ON. I was receiving great pleasure from the magnificent light that was casting itself over the fields of wheat. The setting sun gave off such a golden light it was breathtaking! I was also aware that this scene was being enhanced by the intense black cloud that was forming in the south east.

To my wonder, a large Rainbow formed in the sky ahead of me. It was so large and close that, when I began to take pictures of it, I could only include half of it at a time.

I was not able to easily get out of my vehicle due to a funny incident that had happened earlier that day. So I took pictures from where I sat in the driver's seat with the window open.

What had caught my attention next was that I could clearly see the Rainbow's reflection against the stand of trees. During my childhood and teenage years when I saw a Rainbow, it would end in a forest of trees with no visible reflection.

So I began taking pictures of the scene from all angles. It began to rain. This did not stop me!

With my digital camera I could also stop to check out how the pictures were showing. I observed the ones with the rain and I suddenly realized I was looking at hundreds of Light Orbs!

I had one very specific photograph, with hundreds of orbs, enlarged. There were also two orbs of a different shape visible. The day I picked it up from the photography studio there happened to be a placement student and her teacher present.

The teacher mentioned something about the photograph. I showed him the picture and shared that the transparent disc-life objects were Orbs of Light. He said something like, "Oh, those discs are how the camera responded to the rain."

"Hmm..." I said, and then I asked, "Well then, how would the camera have taken those two orbs by the tree in the field?"

The two Orbs of Light in question were not disc-shaped. They were both hexagonal. The teacher had no explanation as to how that happened, as the camera would not have been able to perform such a task!

To me, this verifies that these orbs are more than the camera's technology responding to the rain.

One other thing that was very significant to me that day was that I was totally in a place of childlike joy! I have since observed that, when I am in total joy or people are this way, the Light Orbs seem to appear more readily.

Many people have seen this picture and have no explanation as to why it looks like this. There are people who believe they too are looking at Light Orbs. I have taken numerous pictures when it was not raining that have Light Orbs in them.

Do you believe "Light Orbs" are real? Have you seen them before in pictures?

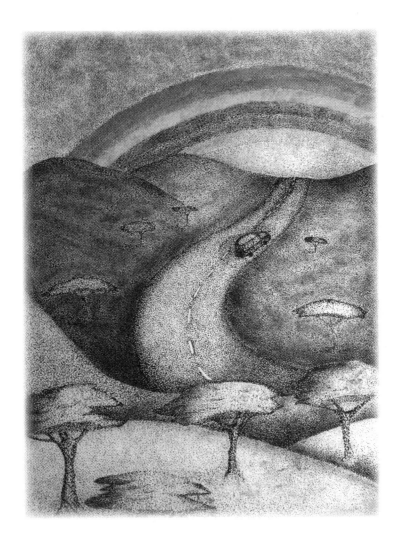

RAINBOW MAGIC

Little did I know that I was going to tap into the Rainbow Fairy Realm on an excursion from Costa Rica to Nicaragua!

In February of 2009, I was invited to travel to Costa Rica by a friend who was considering buying land there. Before leaving Canada, I had received information that I was to find a specific stone carving that would have a significant meaning for me. It was also made clear to me that I was to travel to a warm tropical region.

Once we arrived in Costa Rica, my friend shared that she wanted to check out St. Helena, Costa Rica and the country of Nicaragua. We first travelled by van to St. Helena. We were surprised at how the local people were treated by the visitors. It seemed to us the local people were being treated like second class citizens. This helped my friend rule out this area of Costa Rica for a land purchase.

When we wanted to arrange for transportation to Nicaragua, we realized we were challenged by our limited knowledge of Spanish. We met a young man who had excellent English and Spanish.

The young fellow was travelling to the same place we wanted to go, an Island on Lake Nicaragua called Ometepe Island. There are some ancient stone carvings on it, which was significant for me. Back home I was told to find a stone carving that would have a message in it for me.

In the first two weeks of the trip, I had not seen any stone carvings that resonated with me. I actually stood outside the home we were staying at and put out a call to the Universe that, if there in fact was such a stone somewhere, I would be taken to it.

The following morning we were on our way in a van that was full of people. My friend and I had taken the back seat and I was grateful to be by a window. We travelled along a very rough winding road to the border. We bounced around a lot.

At one point, I observed a Rainbow in the distance. It held my attention, as I wondered if I might see where it ended. Much to my surprise, the road wound around in such a way that we actually drove right under the arch of the Rainbow! Wow, I had never experienced anything quite like that before!

A few minutes later I saw another Rainbow. I was really pleased to see another one. As we drew nearer, I wondered, "Will we drive under it?" Sure enough that is exactly what we did! I did not know if my friend had seen this phenomenon; however, I was very intrigued!

As the van continued on its way, a third Rainbow appeared in the distance! This was simply amazing!

I shared with my friend what I had already seen, and that there was another Rainbow up ahead. We drove under this third Rainbow. It felt to me like I had entered the Fairy Realm! This was totally magical!

To this day, I have not experienced anything like this. Who knows, anything is possible!

I did find the stone that had much meaning to me. It was a large Sun carved in stone, exactly as I had drawn the Sun since my childhood!

Perhaps we need to keep our eyes open and see what magical experiences and sightings the Universe can show us!

Have you ever experienced going under a Rainbow? If you ever went under three Rainbows like I did, what do you imagine was being shown to you?

Sun Stone Carving From Ometepe Island, Nicaragua

Live With Joy in Your Heart!

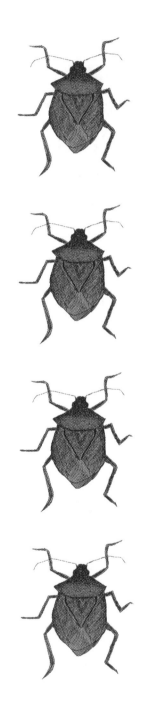

STINK BUGS IN THE SPRING

I was helping my Dad prepare the cottage for use after a long winter. On one particular day, I was cleaning the inside. There were many insects that had found their way into the cottage.

One of the first activities I do is to get as many of the living insects including Stink Bugs outside. I was doing my best to do this before vacuuming. I was imaging that if they continued to come inside, they would be killed. Of course they had a choice.

I had managed to save a number of the Stink Bugs that were downstairs. The ones upstairs were not easy to pick up, as they seemed to cling to the window sill.

There were jobs that needed to be done downstairs on the main level. I went downstairs to attend to them. As I worked at cleaning, I gave the image to the Stink Bugs upstairs that they needed to come down and be on the carpet. This way I could more easily carry them outside. And I also conveyed that, if they stayed inside, they left me no choice but to vacuum them up.

I busied myself with cleaning in the kitchen. After about 10 minutes, I stopped my work to look into the living room. There were now a number of Stink Bugs on the carpet. I took them all outside. I put out one more call to any more living ones upstairs to come down, pronto!

Well that is what they did! When I went back upstairs, all the living Stink Bugs were gone. I was happy for them and pleased that my visualization had worked!

All in a day's envisioning!

Have you ever explored talking to nature? Do you think the bugs understood the mental pictures I gave them?

fun

F U N

Full Understanding Now

(Bruce M.)

THE CURIOUS FRUIT FLY

I am aware that many people often think of the Fruit Fly as an annoying pest. Anyway, this is what I grew up thinking of them.

Then a few years ago I did my best to stop killing them; however, I also did not want them in my home. I created a simple device that allowed their survival for the most part and I did not have them in my home.

In more recent years, I have become far more aware of potential information I might receive if I pay attention and observe the natural world. The Fruit Fly being one of these observable notations.

Perhaps there is far more going on and there is a message that is coming from these insects. I slow down and allow myself to "listen" more inwardly, thus heightening my intuitive awareness.

This is especially apparent when one flies out of the closet as soon as I open the door or I see a few in the bathroom rather than by the fruit.

Recently, I experienced this when one was flying around me for no apparent reason. It reminded me that someone was trying to get hold of me. I sensed to check my phone and sure enough there was a message that required an immediate response

Years ago, I heard about people who were very connected to Planet Earth and received information from it. Some were able to talk and hear messages of information.

Now I am aware that more and more I will say, "Hello" to the natural world from insects to trees to wind to rain. I feel more attuned and sometimes more balanced and connected than I have felt in the past.

I am also aware that this awakening will continue as I experience my life in new ways.

Fruit Flies too may give us information.

What is your perception of this experience?

THE RINGING PHONE MESSAGE

Just this morning something out of the ordinary took place that, for me, seemed both interesting and unusual.

I had arrived in the kitchen just before my Mom came in the front door.

A few moments later, Mom's phone began to ring. She picked it up and said the usual response of "Hello." Pause... "Hello, Hello." There seemed to be no one at the other end.

After a few seconds, Mom turned off the phone. She commented that it must be a telemarketer calling. It often is when she receives this type of call. She was in a hurry and realized she had mere moments before she needed to be heading off to her exercise class.

Mom went on her way out the door. A few minutes later, her phone rang again. It appeared to be a local number so I did not respond. Whoever was calling could leave a Message.

Within moments, I sensed that there was a call or Message for me on my phone. I thought it strange that, if there was, I had not heard it ring. All the same, I went to my phone to discover the ringer had been turned off.

Sure enough, someone had called and left a Message. It was from a special friend of mine. I realized that the call had come in right at the time my Mom's phone had rung.

The Message was heart-felt and most touching. I was so glad to hear it as soon as I did, for it helped to set my day forward.

The Message inspired me to write about the Ringing Phone and to share more stories and insights I have experienced with my life so far.

I remember pondering that it was very unusual that Mom had left her phone behind. Had she not, the ringing of her phone would not have been there to prompt me to check my phone.

It is both fun and fascinating how much the Universe is really communicating with us....if we pay more attention!

As of late, I am really choosing to be more intuitively aware than ever before and to also do better at observing information while listening how best to respond. This whole area really fascinates me!

Does it interest you and are you intrigued to explore this further?

TRUSTING IN THE VISION

The other day I was contemplating adding another story to, "Stories From The Heart: The Ladybug Wish". At that moment, I was gently finger combing my hair before applying a brush to it.

While I was thinking about this story, my hair seemed to release the tangles with ease. Then, as I pondered not putting the story in, I observed an immediate change in my hair.

Knots appeared to form. In fact, one knot presented in such a way that it was not going to "comb" out with ease.

I gently reconsidered putting the story in, and that knot simply transformed into nothing!

The story I was considering putting in began several years ago when I planned an excursion to Lake Superior. I was going to collect stones to add to the heated stones collection I use to enhance massage therapy sessions.

During those years, I was in the process of learning to discern the difference between a vision and a daydream. I was also learning to trust what I was shown. I will emphasize "trust" again.

One day a few weeks before I was to go on my trip to Lake Superior, I observed a vision as a movie in my mind. In this movie, I was driving towards Lake Superior. On the left side of the road, I would see a large black bird. When I got closer to it, I would recognize it to be the body of a Turkey Vulture.

On the opposite side of the road from the Turkey Vulture was a clump of bushes and trees. It was in amongst these bushes and trees that I was guided to go look for the body of a Bear.

I sensed that when I found the Bear I was to take it with me.

"I must be crazy to dream this!" I was thinking at the time.

I remember wondering if this was my imagination or a vision.

"A Bear of all things!" I exclaimed to myself. "It would be really awesome to bring back a Bear to give to Uncle!" (The Bear is very special to Uncle who was my mentor and teacher.)

"A Bear! How would I even be able to lift or move it in the first place?!", I pondered in awe.

I chose not to say anything to anyone. Just in case it was a daydream or my imagination gone wild!

As it turned out, this was neither a daydream nor a wild imagination. I did actually find the Turkey Vulture on the road where I was shown. Across the road was the clump of bushes and trees I had seen in the vision.

The moment came for me to go across the road to search for the Bear. I hesitated.

I turned about, returned to my vehicle and drove on towards Lake Superior. Even though I convinced myself that I would look on my return trip, I never did.

Perhaps I did not trust enough. Even when I was being shown in this reality that what I saw in my vision was coming to fruition.

I remember suggesting to myself that, if I looked and the Bear was not there, I would be disappointed. I may also not have trusted my future visions.

You may be thinking, had I looked and found the Bear, I would definitely have trusted in my visions more readily. This is also possibly true. Well, perhaps you are correct!

What would you have done if this had been your dream or imagination coming true? Would you have been way too curious and had a look anyway? I want to imagine that you might be curious enough!

This story is a reminder to me to trust more. Today I realize that, when I receive visions, I listen and discern. If I am prompted to explore, I do.

Do you ever have visions or are you shown things? Have they come into reality for you? Is there something you have learned about yourself when you have had these experiences?

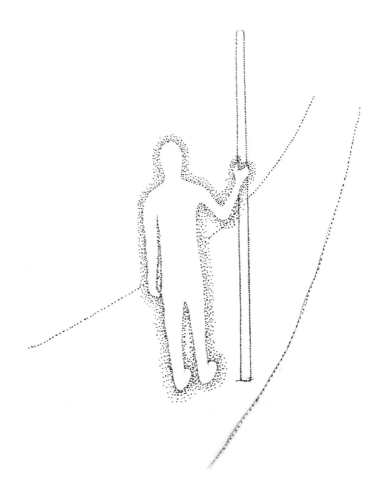

WHO AM I REALLY?

A voice said, "Are you ready?"

My reply was, "Yes."

One day I was driving towards the building where I rent space. I found myself observing a dialogue that appeared to be in my mind. It felt as if this was outside and to my left. Mind you, not in the dimension we presently perceive in. It was similar to watching a movie.

I saw myself standing, holding onto a pole with my right hand while I was waiting for something to happen. It was as though I was going to get on a bus and I was waiting at the bus stop.

The only thing was, I really did not have any form. It was more a sense of form. I heard, or felt a dialogue, as if I was really there and I was speaking with someone.

I heard myself ask, "So, do we still need to go down the birth canal to get to Planet Earth?"

"Yes.", Someone replied.

"Hmmm.....you would think we would have come up with another way to get to Earth by now.", I said.

The reply I heard or felt was, "Not yet; however, you did volunteer for this lifetime."

"Yes, I did. And to think that we need to re-remember who we are and what we are here for. A person may be an adult by then - in Earth years that is." I expressed my awareness.

At that point, I allowed myself to feel the conscious mind from "the place of all knowing". Coming to Planet Earth was wonderful and would be so enriching.

There I was at the "bus stop" waiting as a "being of conscious vibration" for the precise moment that my spirit would enter the avatar body. The woman who carried this body to full term would then birth me onto Planet Earth. It was like coming in a spaceship from a distant location to land.

At this particular moment, in the time space continuum, I had volunteered to go to Earth. Even as a volunteer I would need to re-remember who I am and what I am about.

I also knew that everything was fine. I knew my purpose was about learning to live in joy from a child-like perspective. It may take many "perceived" human years to come to fruition.

What if this actually happened? Have you ever considered that perhaps your soul-self had conversations with Creator before coming to Planet Earth? There are many stories already that seem to imply this. When it comes down to it though, it is really whether you believe this is a possibility. You have the right to decide your truth for yourself.

WHO GOT CAUGHT THAT DAY?

One late spring day, I traveled to a community that has property bordering the Eramosa River. I chose a lovely setting to view the river from a panoramic perspective while sitting in such a way that I was not visible from the river.

This simply seemed like the natural place to set up for weaving. I set up the cast iron lantern stand that also serves the purpose of holding my weaving project.

I settled into the seat and took a few moments to quiet my mind and to absorb the wonderful nature scene: from the river bubbling over the rocks, to the gentle breezes, to the rustling leaves in the trees, to the hum of nearby bees, and the vibrant heat on my shoulders from the sunlight. Hmmm....nice.

I enjoy weaving in a natural setting so the energies of nature may be included in the weave. However, the finger weave design I was working with that day was quite complex and required my focused attention.

Within a few minutes, I began to hear voices and wondered where they were coming from. They were not from the buildings that were behind me. These voices seemed to come from my forward right side. That is the river! How can this be?

Well, I decided to be patient and wait. Sure enough, the voices became louder. They were coming from the river and moving upstream. There were two men, and one was doing most of the talking. Actually, with the water in their midst, I was able to hear his conversation with his friend clearly.

He shared with his friend that this was the very best fishing place he had found. He said he "always" caught Fish here!

They paused to put a pail down and then worked together to set up the net to catch the Fish. Then they waited.

The net was set up from the small island in the river towards the side of the bank where I was.

Once I realized what their intention was, I mentally put a call out to the Fish that might be swimming downstream that day. In my mind I showed the men in the river with the net to this side of the island. If it was a good day for them to die and become food for another, then to come on down the river.

If, however, it was not, I sent out pictures of the Fish staying upstream in deep pools or swimming downstream to the left of the Island.

I waited.

After about 5 to 10 minutes, the man in charge went to the net. I observed him picking out a few small things from the net and place them in the pail. I figured it was meant to be for some Fish to give their lives that day.

They waited some more.

The man checked the nets. There was nothing this time.

I observed him wander upstream and stop at some rocks jutting out of the river. He looked around, scratched his head and waited. He actually looked a little confused or perplexed. The man went back to the nets and checked them again. Still nothing.

He said to his friend that this had never happened before. He just could not understand it! He always caught Fish here!

They gathered up the net and what was in the pail was returned to the river. So if there were little Fish caught, they continued to live too!

When I was sure the two men were gone, I put out the visual signal of "all clear" and continued with my weaving.

What do you think happened? Were there no Fish in the river or did my imaging give them another choice that day?

All is

Well

In All Ways, Shapes and Forms...

ALONG THE RIVER

I was looking for the materials to make a Medicine Wheel based on Uncle's instructions. I required some Dogwood and understood that it grew near wet areas, like a river.

On a weekend I set aside to do some exploration, I visited some property that belonged to a member of my family. I knew that this was a great location to find what I sought, as the property borders a river.

Into my knapsack went the plant book, scissors, pocket knife, water shoes, tobacco, snacks and a towel. I followed the path along the river until I found the way to reach it.

There were two bushes in question. The best and easiest point to see these bushes was to actually get into the river. I was grateful that this side of the river was quite shallow. I took off my hiking boots, socks and put on the water shoes. In I plunged.

I was standing in the river wading up to my knees in a T-shirt, rolled-up jeans, a hat on my head and a purple knapsack on my back. Just as I had started to move towards the first bush, I heard the sound of paddles from a canoe.

To this day, I chuckle as I wonder what the two men in the canoe thought when they went past me in the river. I am sure I was a sight to be seen!

This river is very popular to canoeists and kayakers. Upstream from this property are two bridges for drop-off. People may choose a 2 or 4 hour excursion based on which bridge they are dropped-off from.

Well, on my way again, I neared the first bush. I reached into my knapsack for the book. I discovered that the bush I thought might be Dogwood was just that, so I did not bother to explore the other bush.

As I moved closer, I first heard a sound.

"Hmmm....sounds like buzzing."

Indeed it was, for there in the bush were many Honey Bees collecting nectar from the flowers. I hummed again as I pondered what to do while I placed my knapsack on the bank and took out the items I would need.

I definitely did not want to stick my hands in the bush and disturb the Bees, while at the same time I had no idea how long I would need to wait for them to leave. The Bees might leave and come at different times.

So I decided to ask them, if they might leave while I collected some of the branches. I expressed that I did not want to disturb or hurt them. As I asked, I closed my eyes to concentrate on what I was focusing on and asking. I must say that I was surprised indeed when I opened my eyes. The Bees were gone. All of them!

Next, I asked permission from the bush to have a few of its branches, and placed tobacco down in gratitude. In the Native tradition I was learning, when we ask for something from Planet Earth, we are to give something in return. Hence the tobacco was gifted as a thank you for a few branches from the bush.

I checked the branches, looking for the long straight ones. I took only what I needed which was 3 or 4. This, however, did take some time, and I figured that a good 15-20 minutes had gone by.

When I was ready, I thanked the bush again and put out the Message to the Bees to return as I was finished. Again to my surprise, there they were buzzing and collecting the nectar almost as if they had not left at all.

At the time it felt as though, for those few minutes, I was getting the branches from the Dogwood bush that either I had time-shifted or the Bees had. I never saw or heard them leave or return. I found this very Interesting.

What do you think took place here?

Work

WORK
Wonderful Opportunity Requiring Kindness

Mmmm...sounds like Fun!
(Heather O.)

THE CARDINAL THAT SAW
ITS OWN REFLECTION

There once was a Cardinal that lived in the vicinity of the family cottage. This Cardinal had discovered it could see another Cardinal every time it looked into something that reflected its image.

One might figure the windows of the cottage will do just that. So it makes sense that some of the time the Cardinal might see a reflection of itself when it was flying by a window. This is especially possible when it flies by a large window, like the one at the south side of the cottage.

What surprised me was that it also had discovered the windows and side mirrors of the vehicles we were driving in.

This Cardinal was fearless! It did not seem to really notice that we were in the car or care if we were getting out of the car.

There was a slight problem here because there were no other Cardinals in the area. The more it attacked the windows or the mirrors, the more the attacker seemed to attack it. The bird did not realize that it was seeing its very own reflection! Cardinals can be quite territorial. This was new to me.

Now some years later I find myself remembering this bird and its behaviour.

In the world I am learning about or shall I say remembering, what I send out will be reflected back. Have you ever reflected about what goes out may come back to you? If a person reflects out anger and frustration, she may soon find this being reflected back to her. Have you ever experienced this? It may not necessarily be like the same situation that you were in. However, the vibration of what is sent out will come back. I have observed this time and time again.

When we give out a joyful, peaceful and happy vibration it seems to me that we keep seeing it all around us! If someone we are with is not feeling the same as us, we may choose how we want to respond.

It is my preference to be calm, grounded and joyful within. ~ This vibration will naturally then stream outwards.

Life has taken on a different perspective. I am training myself to be perceptive of how I respond to life around me. With intention to understand more fully that what is given out can and will reflect back. Sometimes it may be quick and at other times over a longer period.

As you read these last 4 paragraphs, I invite you to put yourself into them as though you are writing the insights.

Does this change how you may experience your life and how you may respond to situations in your life? Something to reflect on...

CIRCLE OF HERONS

Years ago, my Mom and I would take my young children for a holiday at a cottage. One of our favourite activities was to go to a local beach. It was on Lake Huron, near Chantry Island.

This Island was uninhabited by humans with the exception of whoever was in charge of the lighthouse. I believe today it works without a human living on the site. So uninhabited by humans; however, fully populated by shore birds!

Over the years, members of my family have seen numerous Herons flying to or from Chantry Island.

On this one vibrant sunny afternoon, I was on the beach basking in the heat after a cooling swim. Even my children were resting quietly.

I was on my towel gazing skyward. Usually I have something over my eyes. This time I did not. I remember looking up and seeing something I had never seen before. I wondered if I was actually dreaming this. So I asked my Mom to look up and to tell me if she saw anything. If so, what did she see? Well she looked up and kept looking up for a bit.

My Mom has been an avid birder for many years. If anyone should know what I was seeing, she would know for sure!

"Yes." she said, "you are seeing correctly. Great Blue Herons do not do that kind of activity. As you saw them first, the message is for you."

What we both observed were three Great Blue Herons flying in a close circle very, very high in the sky!

Herons usually fly near the water or, yes, above in the sky, but not that high! To fly in a circle with 3 together is just not a usual Heron activity.

Even to this day, I am in awe of the memory of this experience. I am aware that the Heron is very special to my Mom. Several years later I have observed it is especially connected to one of my children. I am also now aware that the Great Blue Heron is a guide and teacher to me.

Still the spiral of the circle: It may be as simple as representing the circle of life. When I was reflecting about this memory recently, I saw the image of body, mind and spirit. Then in my heart-mind I asked, "What about 'emotion'?" I heard or sensed... "It is all around us."

If you were to view such a sight at the beach or on a walk someday, what do you sense is the message for you? Or is it simply a beautiful sight to behold?

PUDDLES IN THE SNOW

Things are not always what they may appear to be.

One January thaw, my family and I went for a delightful walk. We were enjoying a hike to a waterfall. My children were very young and at times needed help traversing the trail due to the ice and snow.

I enjoyed pointing things out to them like the different animal tracks. We saw dog and deer tracks. It was fun for my children to figure out what created the tracks.

"These are different tracks. Who made them?"

My children suddenly realized I was referring to their boot tracks.

"We made them with our boots!"

They laughed. We laughed with our girls.

This winter day we were enjoying simply being outdoors on a balmy day. In splash pants and light blazers, to boot!

The walk was challenging at times with the combination of ice and snow patches. There were puddles too. It wasn't long before one of my girls had slipped and landed among the puddles.

We reached the waterfall which was more ice than water. With the sun shining, it sparkled with vibrant diamonds of light!

The rest, along with the snacks of cheese, crackers, apples and juice refreshed us. We began our walk back. I remember realizing how different the view was. It was enjoyable and fun to delightfully observe new sights simply from a different view point.

One of these sights was the little puddles. We had continued to see them on the trail to the waterfall.

During our return walk, I suddenly realized the puddles had, through my eyes, transformed into deer tracks. These tracks may have been days old. During a cold spell, they had solidified. With the melt in progress, they had filled with water to become lots of mini puddles.

The whole walk was such an enriching experience! I realized the significance of looking from different points of view. What appeared to be a common puddle was more than we first realized!

It is important to view the world from a variety of angles and not just during a walk. How we relate with people and circumstances can be viewed in the same way.

Can you remember when you thought you saw or heard something only to discover it was something totally different?

When you get the opportunity to go for a walk in nature, for fun you might find something that intrigues you. Perhaps you will look at it from different angles to explore if it does look different. What do you see?

Be Your Joy!

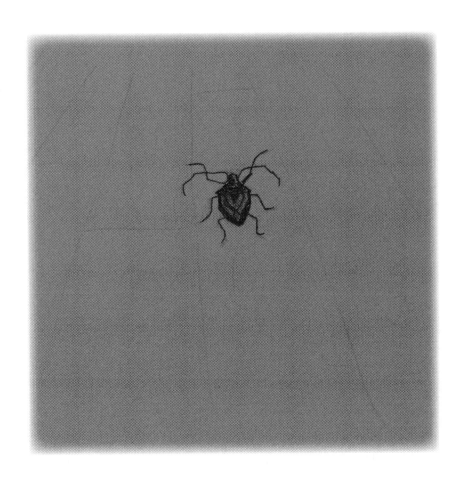

FROM STINK, SHIELD TO CHEVRON BUG

On Tuesday of this week I experienced a number of interesting messages. The first one I noted was the Stink Bug. I observed it on the floor of my bedroom which was facing towards my entrance door. Interestingly, that is the East direction. The second unusual observation I noted was when I arrived downstairs to the level where my vehicle is parked. One of the condo attendants had just finished washing the floor that I had to walk on to get to the car park. The third thing I observed was, when I was going out for my two minute walk between clientele, I heard the Jays calling most distinctly!

So what does this all mean in my life? Are there, in fact, possible messages here to assist me with my day? Is this all a figment of my imagination? Some may say "Yes." Others who have experienced something of these kinds of observations will think or answer differently. And for others, this is intriguing and interesting to explore.

As with the Ladybugs, autumn is a time when the Stink Bugs want to be indoors, especially in our region. However, I have only begun to notice them in these more recent years.

In previous years, the common insects that came in were the Ladybugs. So, seeing the Stink Bug in my room apparently heading towards my door and in the easterly direction, I decided to observe if there was a message here for me!

One of the things that I like about Stink Bugs is their natural shades of brown, and when their wings are folded they look like the chevron weave pattern. Since I love to finger weave, I am most fascinated with their patterns. So I would rather call them the Chevron Bug!

They are also known as Shield Bugs. I have already had some wonderful experiences with this insect, so seeing it again in early autumn at my home intrigued me.

I decided to check out the Totem Message Meaning for the Stink Bug to see if I might receive more insights:

"Heightened intuition, insights, visions, increased sensitively".

What I find most interesting is that I have chosen to be more aware. I have a desire to deepen my intuitive awareness while doing my best to follow with my Heart-Mind. And here is a confirming or an invitation message via the Stink Bug! It was moving forward out the door and also into the East. Both are movements for new learning and growth. New beginnings! I had my confirmation.

Then downstairs I go! I am required to walk on the newly-washed floor as if "the plate has been washed clean. I am stepping out onto new waters of information!"

Later that morning at my work I realized a client was due to arrive in about 15 minutes which meant I had 10 minutes available for a walk. As I headed out, I heard the Jays call loudly.

Over the years, the Jay has been teaching me that things may not be as they appear to be, caution alert or you have forgotten something. When I heard the Jays' call, my first sense was "You do not have enough time to go for the walk." I decided to take this message as a reminder to return sooner.

What I did not know was my client had already arrived, and the Jays' call was "not now for the walk", period.

As it turned out, I was late for my client; however, she did see me and shared she knew I was returning. This was a very beneficial reminder to take heed when time is limited.

What is also intriguing is that this was all from one morning. Messages and wisdom are coming to us all the time.

I also ponder, "Did I create this beforehand to help me in my experience, or is the help coming because I put out the intention and desire for the help?

Are all of these experiences really random happenings?

Did it come in a fun way because we are really meant to enjoy this human experience on Planet Earth?"

I have a pretty strong belief, and I also know this awareness is deepening. I am learning more, or perhaps I am awakening to the knowledge that is already here and I did not realize it until now.

Have you ever considered the concept of receiving a message from a Stink Bug or a Jay? Now this is something for you to think about!

Peace Be With You & Also With You!

MY WEATHER BEACON

I do not remember how many years ago I began to realize that, when I saw a Great Blue Heron, I would generally know the weather that I was going to experience. I had deduced that Herons will, if possible, always fly towards fine sunny weather. This was what I have continued to observe.

For example, while I was driving north one summer, I saw a Heron flying right towards me. It was flying south while I was driving north. I knew we were about to drive into rain.

I mentioned to the friend I was travelling with that we were about to drive into rain. My friend looked surprised and then within about 2 or 3 minutes, sure enough, we were driving in rain! My friend gave me a strange look. At the time I did not feel comfortable enough to speak about what the Heron's flight direction showed me.

A few years later, I was travelling with a different friend from Manitoulin Island on Lake Huron to the mainland. We were travelling together to spend the day at Lake Superior. I planned this trip to collect some smooth black basalt stones. I use heated stones for my massage therapy clients.

While traveling northbound on the Island, I observed a Heron on my right. It was fishing in a small pond. I pondered what that might mean, if anything. At the time my sense was, "Wherever I am, the weather will be sunny." Hmmm... I considered this for a few moments.

Several hours later we arrived at a beach. It felt like this would be a great place to stop. Soon it became apparent I would not find any basalt stones. I did find stones! Lots of small, orange-coloured ones, and I took a few with me.

We had been on the beach about 30 minutes. I observed what appeared to be fog rolling in from the west. It was moving up along the beach towards us. I wondered if the message I sensed from the Heron was incorrect. Then, within minutes, the fog suddenly dispersed and was gone! I deduced the Heron message was very accurate!

The sun had warmed the stones. I took two and held them gently near my friend's low back. She was able to feel their warmth even through the cloth of her shirt!

We had a delightful few hours at the beach. Unbeknownst to us there was more to come on our travels home!

One was a Bear crossing the road with a Raven flying above it. A little later, I saw something else unusual. It looked like a large calf. I did a wide turnaround. When I drove close to the place where I saw the animal, a large

Black Bear was standing up on its hind legs. It popped its head through a bush that was near the edge of the road. This bear was just as curious as we were!

Sometimes when I wonder about the weather or I am not consciously thinking about the weather, I will see a Heron. I can be quite sure what the weather will be like. Especially in the direction I am travelling! I will note here that this is for 3 seasons of the year. Usually we do not see Herons in our winters.

Please know that this is what I have experienced with the Heron. For each of you it may be the same or different! I find it both fun and enriching to observe the natural world and listen for messages. There often are.

What we need to be doing is listening, paying attention, and observing! Often the message is to learn something about ourselves!

Are you eager to try it?

All is Well in Every Way,
Shape, and Form.

Do you see the bird created by the clouds?

HAWKS IN FLIGHT

There was a time when I enjoyed going out for a drive to explore the land. On one particular day, I wondered about finding some unwanted sticks of wood suitable for burning in a fire and some cedar branches. I was also interested in finding swan feathers.

I had not planned to go to the store to purchase these items. It was more about going out for a drive and observing what might be presented to me.

I did not have any particular direction in mind; however, I found that I was driving on Paisley Road and signaled my vehicle to turn left on Whitelaw Road (Guelph, ON).

As I drove up the hill along the well-travelled paved road, I observed the forest of deciduous trees to my left and the field of grain growing to my right.

A Hawk flew up from the field. It was at that moment I decided to follow the Hawks that day. I drove in the direction the Hawk was flying until I saw another one, and then drove in the new direction.

This first Hawk I observed was flying southeast, so this is the direction I took. Some minutes later, I saw another Hawk. It was flying west. I drove west at the next possible turn. It was wonderful to be carefree with my time so I could be in the moment of my experience.

It was a great day. The air was warm, and it was sunny. A few days earlier, a storm had moved through the area. I observed some branches of trees on the ground.

About 45 minutes later, I suddenly observed some sticks of wood - the size I was hoping to find - on the left side of the road. I stopped and got out to check them. They were just what I was looking for. The sticks were older and weathered, however not rotted yet. There were about 5 or 6 pieces. That is all that I gathered.

From the Native tradition I was learning, I was to honour the gift received. I placed some tobacco on the ground in thanksgiving and for the exchange.

Along this same road, I also observed a pond with swans swimming on it. There were both black and white swans. I was happy to see them; however, I did not stop as I sensed I was simply to enjoy viewing them.

When another Hawk appeared, I turned my vehicle to follow it. Several minutes later, I saw another Hawk and followed in the direction it flew.

At one point, I was driving very slowly along a gravel road with a Hawk flying directly in front of me over the road. It was both amazing and exhilarating to experience! After a few minutes, the Hawk changed direction. It flew to the right of me. I followed in this direction at the next possible turn in the road.

I found that I was drawing closer to a small 4-corner community. There was a church to my left (west) and the road jogged to the right slightly before heading north again. As I drove towards this road heading north, I observed that a fairly large cedar tree had fallen down. It was to the left of me on the shoulder of the road. There were a few branches in reach. With ease, I collected some.

After placing down some tobacco with thanks to the cedar and also to the Hawks I had followed that day, I slowly headed home. It was a great day! I had found and seen all that I wanted.

I was grateful for the Hawks' guidance and for this delightful adventure!

Perhaps this is something you might do... follow a Hawk and observe where it takes you.

Joy is in the Heart!

THE JAYS ARE CALLING

One year while I was visiting Manitoulin Island, I began to pay attention to messages from the Jay!

I distinctly remember heading towards Uncle's summer home, when I observed the sudden burst of blue as four Blue Jays took flight. They were calling out loud and clear, "Jay, Jay, Jay, Jay!"

They were making sure that I saw and heard them! For me the initial feeling was that something was off, not right, or amiss. Well I was in a hurry, so I did not stop long to reflect what that might mean!

When I arrived at Uncle's place, we spoke for a few moments. Uncle seemed upset and agitated. He then went silent and left. I perceived at that moment something was wrong.

I quickly left and went to the Sacred Fire to offer tobacco with a prayer for Uncle.

There is a Ceremony for the start of a powwow, and an important aspect of this ceremony is the start of a special fire known as the "Sacred Fire". It is kept burning until the closing ceremony of the powwow. There are other special ceremonies that may take place at the Sacred Fire like The

Sunrise Ceremony. It is a fire that one may offer prayers for another as I did that day for Uncle.

After that, I did not notice the Jays much! Then a few years later when I was planning to make a major life change, I began to observe the Jays calling out strong. It seemed almost uncanny to me that when I was out in nature and thinking about my plans, the Jays showed up.

Like when I was observing sunrises and strongly imagined my new life, I would see a large flock of Jays arrive and call out. Another time, a Jay hopped out of a nearby tree. It called until I stopped to observe it.

"Hmmm, what caused it to call so strongly? What was I actually thinking about, when I saw and heard the Jay? Oh yes, I was thinking about my plan to live in a new place."

Over time I have come to realize when I hear the Jay calling I have a sense of caution alert, or things are not as they may appear to be, or perhaps I have forgotten to attend to something.

A friend of mine shared once that Jay to her meant royalty and all is well with her decisions. The Jay will possibly give us similar or different messages.

Have you ever wondered what the Jay's message may be for you? Perhaps the most important thing to do is to simply observe and listen.

♥

$2 + 1 + 5 =$ ____

♥

$5 + 10 + (2 \times 7) =$ ____

♥

$2*(8-X)^2 + 36 \div 3 = 30$

$X =$ ____

MANIFESTING & MATH

Tonight I find that once again I sense the keen desire to write. I wonder, "What do I write?"

Years ago, I heard or sensed from an inner place, "Write about your childhood, and write about things from the heart." Recently, I sensed, "Write to share your insights and the way you experience the world from day to day."

A friend recently shared with me that I am amazing at manifesting. What my friend meant is that I am now beginning to manifest the things I want into my life more consciously. It has taken me many years to develop the awareness that what I am experiencing in my daily life, I have already manifested. Even if it is something I prefer not to experience.

In more recent years, I am now beginning to observe "unwanted experiences or situations". I have begun to ponder their presence from a different perspective than I did in the past. I think, "Why would I even want to create this into my experience?"

Granted, I fully realize that this is a continual process, and I am learning daily to listen, observe and learn from a more neutral place. Sometimes it is much easier than at other times.

Like earlier today, another friend was sharing his perspective on the American school system that changed in the early 1900's. The emphasis is no longer on achievement of the basic fundamentals like, reading, writing and arithmetic.

Now it is about creating a rounded balance for students. Hence, music, sports and the arts are included and are perceived to be equally valued as the traditional academic subjects.

My friend disapproved of this change. He believed that the school system should still be teaching only the core fundamental courses.

As much as I was attempting to listen to my friend's point of view, I found myself tensing up. My friend picked up on this immediately, even though I had not said anything.

He said, "What is your point of view on this, as I can feel you tensing?" Indeed, it was loud and clear, and the vibration was totally apparent!

In my experience, while attending school from public to high school, I struggled for just about every mark or grade I got.

Frankly, I thought I was not smart. Not anything like my older siblings who seemed to breeze through school and do well at anything that was presented to them, from academics to sports to music to the arts. It seemed royally unfair to me at the time! What I did not realize is that my gifts lay elsewhere.

I excelled in many of the "hands-on" courses...with great ease, while I was highly challenged with the core academic courses.

It felt as though I was just not ready to learn them. Somehow I missed getting the foundation and I would become very lost and confused. This was especially apparent when new information was added. I guess I was most terrified of Math (especially problem solving).

Of course, there is more. Basically I did not comprehend what the teachers were instructing. Some thought I was not paying attention. From my perspective, I was doing my very best to be attentive. I shared some of this with my friend.

I realized that for all the clearing and healing that I had done over the years, I was still emotionally sensitive about math. I expressed my frustration at wanting to learn and understand what was being taught, to no avail.

Hence, I now want to learn to understand math and be at ease with it. I realized earlier today that it is fun to learn. In so doing I am empowering myself to reach new heights with confidence. I feel that perhaps I am now ready to learn the foundation and continue to propel myself forward with renewed zest. After all, I am a good luck manifestor!

It is also interesting that there is the belief that knowledge is already within us. So the thrill is in finding the simplest way to extract this knowledge and utilize it for more creative experiences.

What is your perspective on this? Is it worthwhile for you to explore?

Play with Joy!

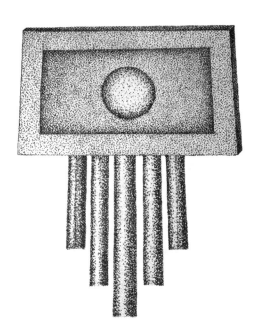

MESSAGING FROM A DOOR CHIME

Recently, I have found doorbells to be able to give messages.

"What?" You may say. "How can that be?"

Well, here is my story and you can decide for yourself.

In the late spring of 2014, my Mother shared that the doorbell did not work well. She thought a new one might make a difference. I went out and purchased a new doorbell.

This one happened to include several doorbell chimes with it. There was the traditional ding dong chime, a fancy musical chime, a Christmas chime – Jingle Bells, a Christian chime and the American Anthem chime. (Strange, where is the Canadian Anthem chime?)

We chose the fancy musical chime to sound when someone comes to our door.

It worked like a charm when people came to our door. It worked so well that, even when our neighbour's bell went off, ours joined in! There was the time that I was playing a game with my Mom and the doorbell sounded. I asked my Mom why she had changed the chime. She said she hadn't.

"Oh, really?"

Well, what we were now hearing of all things was the American Anthem chime! I went to the door. No one was there. Then I felt prompted to check my phone. Sure enough, there was a message from my friend who happens to be an American!

"Wow, I thought!" he can give off strong vibrations even from across the border and into Canada!

Now this doorbell seems to have a character of its own. Most of the time though, it does ring like it is designed to do when someone is at the door.

A few months ago my Mom and I were getting ready to go for a walk with my grandson, who was bundled up snug and warm in the carriage. We were just getting our coats and boots on for the outing when the doorbell began to chime. Mom said that there would be no one there.

Of course no one was "physically" there! Well, didn't the door bell continue to sound through all the possible chimes that it has!

Mom shared that it was helping to entertain our little one while we were getting ready. My grandson was happy and smiling and we began to laugh and laugh! Such fun!

Oh, and it stopped chiming when we reached for the door too! Our smiles continued for quite some time as we left and yes, no one was there.

Several weeks later, the door chimed again while my Mom and I were playing some games. Mom said there would be no one there.

"How did she know this in the first place?", you may wonder.

We live in a condominium, and if people are at the front door they must ring the phone in order to come in. If it is someone in the building my Mom knows, they will call her before coming.

Our unique doorbell chime has rung countless times before, and when Mom goes to the door no one is there. Most of the time, when it chimes, Mom ignores it.

In the evenings when I am home, I will go to the door to see who has arrived. If no one in physical form is there, I will invite in our Angel Friends and Ancestor Relatives who have come to visit. Yes, I realize they can arrive at anytime and by any means. Well, apparently we have some who enjoy ringing the doorbell too!

So, the door chimed one evening once again when my Mom and I were playing some games.

I arrived at the door to observe that it was not yet locked. We had both figured the door was already locked. I was very grateful for the doorbell chiming on this particular evening, as I then locked the door after inviting our Angels to come in!

Have you ever had an experience like this before or something similar to it?

Our lives can be so powerful and enriching.
If your life is this way already, great!
For me, it is simply a joy to share!
(Heather O.)

What do you see....a cloud; an angel; a unicorn...?

CLOUD WATCHING

Do you remember lying on your back outside in the summer? Did you watch fluffy clouds rolling by? As you observed the clouds you creatively imagined some of them looking like birds, animals or objects. It was fun to see what the next cloud shape might look like.

I fondly remember doing this during my childhood. Cloud watching is still fun for me today. Indeed we are young enough to do this at any age!

Over the years I have begun to observe other shapes that appeared in cliffs and stone structures. They were naturally created by the earth.

I have observed such amazing sites. I especially remember the time I attended a sacred journey to Newfoundland and the group I was with visited the Fjords (Western Brook Pond, in Newfoundland's Gros Morne National Park).

First we were bussed to a parking lot. We were required to walk to the place where we met a ferry. It would take us into the fjords.

Originally, I am told, this fresh water pond (lake) had ocean access. Whale bones have been found deep in these fjords as one proof that this once was ocean-connected.

The Shaman in charge began to share that images may be observed in these rocks. I had already seen some. It was wonderful to have the Shaman point out other images that I had not observed!

Even after I arrived home, I continued to see more images in the pictures I took of these magnificent rock formations!

For me, the universe of the natural world has opened more fully and exquisitely! As I observe mountains and cliffs, I see giants looking skyward. Almost as if they are the keepers of the skies.

So, from clouds to hills, to land formations, I invite you to observe what images you see. Observe if these images are significant for you. Simply enjoying our natural world can open up our day beautifully.

Take some time to watch the clouds to see what you can see!

THE LADYBUG WISH

I was enjoying a few minutes quiet, reflecting on my day before retiring for some needed sleep.

I had originally figured I would be having a great conversation with my good friend from the USA. He, however, was very busy.

Since opportunities are always presenting themselves, I decided that it was a wonderful evening all the same.

Suddenly something fell or landed – *Plunk* – on my right shoulder! I felt whatever it was land but could not feel anything else. I brushed my hand over my shoulder and out popped a Ladybug!

This one had many black spots on its folded wings. Ah, yes, it is the season for Ladybugs to come indoors as the autumn weather draws cooler. Still what of the Ladybug?

I remember once reading that you should count the spots when a Ladybug lands on you. For every spot you may make a wish. For fun I counted the spots. On one side there were 9 spots! That meant there were 18 in total! This may be an opportunity in the making!

Indeed, Ladybug gifts may be coming my way! Of course, this all depends on one's perspective. I looked for information for any new insights about Ladybugs. Some people also believe Ladybugs bring luck, especially if they land on you. One makes a wish and lets the Universe bring it to them. Patience is needed here.

I pondered what I wanted.

At that particular moment, what I wished for was for my friend in the USA to be very successful with his inventions: One is a wood stove that uses very little wood to create heat and also creates little-to-no smoke emissions; the second is an insert for outdoor boilers that have the same positive results!

Now, what if the boiler does not need to burn wood?

Instead, it can burn tires or trash to create heat for homes and buildings, and there are little-to-no emissions! Indeed, I truly want this wish to come into reality for my friend. He may be able to help us all clean up our landfills!

Imagine that!

It is my hope that this book of stories, Stories From The Heart: The Ladybug Wish, will open up a new wonder for you - to create possibly a deeper appreciation for the natural world we live in and to open us further to new insights of wisdom.

If a Ladybug should land upon you, remember to count the dots and make a wish!

EPILOGUE

It was a great joy and enriching experience to publish this first book, "Stories From The Heart: The Ladybug Wish!

I am in the process of writing my next two books. One will be a children's picture book about the Magic of Christmas and the other book will be a continuation of the Stories From The Heart series.

If you decided to do the math equations from the story, "Manifesting & Math", here are the answers:

1. $2 + 1 + 5 = \underline{8}$
2. $5 + 10 + (2 \times 7) = \underline{29}$
3. $2*(8-X)^2+36 \div 3=30$
   X= 5 or 11

STORY TITLES FOR CUT-OUT GAME

Cut out the titles of the stories in this section of the book. Place them in a bag. Choose one story. See where it takes you.

Crows

Stepping Out

Blowing Angel Kisses

A Pail Full Of Crabs

Wolf Smile

Rainbow Delight

Pot Of Gold

Rainbow & Light Orbs

Rainbow Magic

Stink Bugs In The Spring

The Curious Fruit Fly

The Ringing Phone Message

Trusting In The Vision

Who Am I Really?

Who Got Caught that Day?

Along The River

The Cardinal That Saw Its Own Reflection

Circle Of Herons

Puddles In The Snow

From Stink, Shield To Chevron Bug

My Weather Beacon

Hawks In Flight

The Jays are Calling

Manifesting & Math

Messaging From A Door Chime

Cloud Watching

The Ladybug Wish

ABOUT THE AUTHOR

Heather A. Oliver, RMT lives in Guelph, Ontario. She is the CEO and owner of Healing With Nature's Touch – Holistic Healing Centre located on the beautiful natural grounds of the Ignatius Jesuit Centre, Guelph. Heather has 25 years experience in the Holistic Field. Heather has 3 adult daughters and a grandchild.

www.heatheraoliver.com

Printed in the United States
By Bookmasters